I0605532

THE LITTLE BOOK OF TREES

FELICITY HART

Red Wheel

This edition first published in 2025 by Red Wheel, an imprint of
Red Wheel/Weiser, LLC
With offices at:
65 Parker Street, Suite 7
Newburyport, MA 01950
www.redwheelweiser.com

ISBN: 978-1-59003-588-7
Library of Congress Cataloging-in-Publication Data available upon request

Printed and bound in China
1010 Printing International Ltd
10 9 8 7 6 5 4 3 2 1

This FSC® label means that materials and other controlled sources used for the product have been responsibly sourced.

CONTENTS

✶ INTRODUCTION ✶

For thousands of years, trees have sheltered and nourished us, inspired us and watched over our lives, so it's no wonder that they shape the landscape of our myths and folk tales, too. They stand proudly at the heart of many ancient stories, as symbols of wisdom, fertility, protection and even life itself.

In this book we will explore the magick and mysticism of trees, traveling across the continents and through history to discover the impact nature's gentle giants have had on our culture and picking up some fascinating biological facts about them along the way.

Trees hold a sacred place in many belief systems and are an important focus for rituals and worship. *The Little Book of Trees* includes profiles of tree deities and also looks at the way trees feature in the creation stories of many religions. There's even a chapter on spells and rituals to show you how to weave some tree magick of your own.

At a time when many of us would like to reconnect with the natural world, this little book offers the perfect solution. It will help you tune in to the wonderful energy of trees, rediscover nature's rhythms and get

back to your roots... so let's head off to explore the enchanted forest!

CHAPTER ONE:

TREES IN FOLKLORE

Our relationship with trees has developed over millennia of living alongside them and depending on them for food, fuel, shelter and inspiration. In bygone days, they were the most distinctive feature of an area: the perfect landmark for the traveler, the ideal place for locals to meet in the shade to gossip or sell their goods. A grand old tree was a part of the community to the people who had grown up playing among its branches, and trees were often given names linked to their role: the shearing tree, the trysting tree, the gospel oak.

Trees were (and are) key to our lives, so it's no wonder that generations of rich traditions have grown up around them. In this chapter, we'll delve into some of the fascinating tree folklore and wisdom inherited from our ancestors. We look at the customs and cures associated with different species - and since trees are a central theme in many folk tales, we'll take a moment to discover some of these, too.

THE MAGICKAL ROWAN 

To the ancient Druids, all trees were significant and had different qualities and associations, but the rowan was particularly magickal. It was thought to provide powerful protection against malevolent forces, thanks to the sacred pentagram symbol that appears on each berry.

There are dozens of fascinating superstitions surrounding the rowan, and it was often planted near homes for its protective qualities. The wood would be incorporated into the lintel above the hearth or formed into a cross to be hung over a barn door to keep livestock safe. It was used to make cradles, ploughs, or pegs for cattle. A rowan walking cane would help you see in the dark, and a rowan stick used as a spoon would stop your milk from curdling. You could protect your cows by tying a rowan twig to their tails, and protect your sheep by encouraging them to jump through a rowan hoop. And if you wanted to add a year to your life, you could eat some rowan berries.

✶ A TREE OF REFUGE ✶

In the autumn, the streets of Santa Cruz, Bolivia, are bursting with the pink and white blooms of the toborochi tree. This tree, a relative of the baobab, develops a hollow, swollen trunk as it matures, which is why it's nicknamed "the pregnant tree." The name "toborochi" actually translates as "tree of refuge" since Indigenous people used to shelter in the trees' hollow trunks.

The themes of pregnancy and refuge are combined in a local legend about the tree, which tells of a princess, Araverá, who was pursued through the sky by evil spirits (Añas) after she became pregnant with the child of Colibri, the hummingbird god. The spirits were intent on killing Araverá because they feared her son would be a god-prince who would destroy them. After many months fleeing the spirits, the princess hid inside the trunk of a toborochi tree, where she safely gave birth to her child. Her son grew up to defeat the Añas, but Araverá remained in the tree, and her spirit is displayed every autumn when the trees blossom.

HOW THE BAOBAB CAME TO BE

These solitary trees are an iconic species on the African savannah. It's their upside-down appearance that makes them so distinctive - their canopy looks like a root system rather than branches - and several folk tales describe how this came about.

Along the Zambezi some tribes tell the story of a creator god who objected to the baobab growing in his garden. He seized the tree and threw it out of Paradise. It fell down to earth, landing upside-down, and this is the way it has grown ever since. Another tale describes how the baobab tree went roaming around the garden after God first planted it, so he replanted the tree upside-down to stop it from walking away.

Or perhaps the tree's appearance is down to Hyena. In Namibia, the story goes that God wanted to assign a tree to every animal. The animals gathered to receive their trees, but Hyena was last in the queue. She was so unimpressed with the baobab sapling she was given that she threw it aside, and it landed upside-down.

However the tree came into being, it is certainly a keystone species. Baobabs are a food source for

elephants and baboons, a home to storks and bush babies, and provide sustenance and essential materials for humans who live nearby. It's said that drinking water in which baobab pips have been soaked will give you strength and protection from crocodiles.

The Baobab Amoureux of Madagascar are two trees that have grown twisted around one another. According to Malagasy legend, these trees were two lovers who were forbidden to unite by their rival families. They prayed to their gods to allow them to be together, and their wish was granted. They were transformed into trees, able to embrace one another for all time. Today, many couples visit the trees to seek blessing for their own union.

THE MIGHTY OAK

Sturdy and strong, this stalwart of the countryside is revered as a symbol of resilience; it can withstand all but the worst weathers and live for up to a thousand years. It's no surprise that this king of the forest features in legends wherever it's found. Oaks were associated with Thor, the Norse god of thunder, and the ancient Druids carried out their most sacred ceremonies in oak groves.

A potent gift offered by this tree is the acorn, and carrying one was believed to bring the bearer luck. Young lovers wishing to discover their future could float two acorns together in a bowl: if they moved toward one another, the couple's love would last; if they drifted apart, then so would the couple. Oak galls – rounded growths found on some trees – were also used for divination. Placing them in a bowl of water beneath a child's crib was once a way to tell if they'd been bewitched. Meanwhile, breaking open a gall and examining the creature inside could foretell the fate of the harvest.

HAWTHORN – THE FAIRY TREE

The hawthorn, or May tree, is synonymous with fertility and bursts into frothy white blossom at Beltane (1 May), the pagan festival of birth. It has stood proudly at the heart of May Day celebrations for centuries. Its blossoms were woven into garlands to adorn the maypole, the revelers, and their homes and barns. The trees themselves were also decorated.

Known as "fairy trees," hawthorns were often planted near wells to watch over these sacred places. Sprigs were placed above a baby's crib for good fortune and were also believed to protect against storms at sea. Ill luck would strike anyone who felled a hawthorn, and to this day many are left undisturbed by farmers, particularly in Ireland. Some people believed the blossoms would bring bad luck if brought into the house.

The crown of England was said to be found hanging in a hawthorn tree after the Battle of Bosworth Field. The red haws (berries) and white blossom of the tree made it the perfect emblem for Henry Tudor to incorporate into his heraldic badge, symbolizing the moment he took the crown from Richard III.

✶ HEALING TREES ✶

The healing properties of trees have been harnessed for millennia, and many traditional remedies are still used effectively today. The bark of the cottonwood tree has long been used as an anti-inflammatory in the US. The resin is antiseptic, while the buds and bark were used by many Indigenous tribes for pain relief.

The pharaohs of ancient Egypt were prescribed pine resin to treat breathing problems, and today ongoing studies are investigating the use of pine bark extract to treat asthma sufferers. Sap from the bloodwood tree is still used as an antiseptic by Indigenous Australians, who also pioneered the use of tea tree for treating coughs and eucalyptus to combat colds, fever and stomach problems.

Some remedies, however, are not so popular in modern times. A cure for sick children, common in Britain centuries ago, was to pass them through a split made in the trunk of an ash tree. After the children had been lifted through the gap, the tree would be bound back together. If it healed, it was believed, so would the children, and tokens of gratitude would be left at the foot of the tree. In fact, the ash tree was believed to have

many healing qualities - including treating snake bites and jaundice - and newborn babies were traditionally given a teaspoon of ash sap to promote good health.

Not all tree remedies were pleasant for the patient: an early treatment for chilblains was to beat them with a holly branch, and toothache sufferers were advised to use a nail to make their gum bleed and then hammer the nail into an oak tree to banish their pain. If that seems a little gory, you might prefer to carry a hazelnut in your pocket to cure the pain instead. Meanwhile, carrying a walnut with a spider inside in your pocket was recommended for treating a fever.

JOHNNY APPLESEED

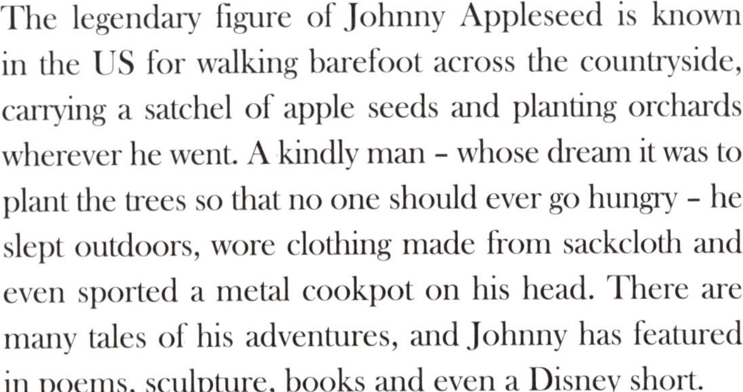

The legendary figure of Johnny Appleseed is known in the US for walking barefoot across the countryside, carrying a satchel of apple seeds and planting orchards wherever he went. A kindly man - whose dream it was to plant the trees so that no one should ever go hungry - he slept outdoors, wore clothing made from sackcloth and even sported a metal cookpot on his head. There are many tales of his adventures, and Johnny has featured in poems, sculpture, books and even a Disney short.

The man who inspired the legend, John Chapman, did indeed walk barefoot across the country, but the trees he planted didn't produce sweet fruit that could be eaten by a hungry passerby. In fact, the sour fruit - known as "spitters," because that's what you would do after taking a bite! - were perfect for making cider, which is what Chapman intended. He owned a franchise of orchards by the time he passed away in 1845. Just one of the trees he planted is still standing today, and at over 180 years old, the tree still bears apples perfect for cider-making.

✶ DOWSING RODS ✶

The tradition of dowsing - using a wooden rod to detect substances hidden below ground - goes back millennia. The first written account is attributed to Herodotus, who described the use of a rod to find water back in the fifth century BCE, but it's likely that our ancestors turned to "water witching" before that. The ability to find a source of underground water would have been highly valued. Dowsing was also used to detect other substances, from precious minerals to buried treasure, and even to follow in the footsteps of thieves.

Dowsing was seen as a form of occultism and was frowned upon by the Catholic Church during the sixteenth century. In Europe, the dowsing woods of choice were hazel and willow, but in the US, peach wood was also used. The dowser would carry a Y-shaped branch and walk across the search area with this held in front of them. It was believed that the rod would be dragged down toward the earth when the target was directly beneath them.

BIRTHING AND BURIAL TREES

Trees are sacred to the people of the 500-plus Indigenous Australian and Torres Strait Islander countries and often play an important role in their birthing and burial rituals. In south-eastern Australia, the Wiradjuri people created *marara*, carved trees that marked the burial place of important members of the community. A large oval of bark was removed from the trunk and elaborate symbolic patterns were carved on the exposed surface of the tree. These *marara* face the site of the burial.

"Birthing trees," often large gum trees, are equally sacred sites where a pregnant woman would retreat to give birth in the shelter of the tree's hollow trunk. (In some areas, this practice continues today.) The new mother and baby might stay within the tree's safe embrace while recovering from the birth, and for some there was a tradition that the baby's placenta would be buried beneath the tree, forming a link between the child and its sacred guardian. This custom goes back over 60,000 years and some trees have seen the birth of over 10,000 babies.

TREE MEDICINE

As well as the many traditional herbal remedies gifted to us by trees, research into some folk cures has led to the development of modern drug treatments. The use of cinchona bark for treating fevers by Indigenous tribes in the Andes led to the mass production of quinine to treat malaria, and white willow bark was described by Hippocrates as an effective painkiller, with the active component, salicin, being developed into aspirin in 1897.

After centuries of use treating digestive complaints, hawthorn extract is proving to be a successful treatment for high blood pressure and chronic heart problems, performing well in clinical trials.

It may seem that the yew tree has little potential for healing: every part of it is poisonous to humans. But extracts from yew clippings can stop the development of cancer cells, and taxane-based drugs are used to combat ovarian, breast and prostate cancers. Meanwhile, extracts from the seeds of the black bean tree, highly toxic unless carefully prepared, are currently being trialed for managing HIV/AIDS.

SAKURA – THE JAPANESE CHERRY BLOSSOM

Sakura trees burst into flower for a week every spring in Japan, and their delicate blossoms have become the country's unofficial national flower. For centuries, this time of year has been celebrated with feasts beneath the trees, where people sip sake and carry out the ritual of *hanami*: gazing at the wonderful display of petals. In ancient times, farmers would make an annual offering under the trees, praying for a bountiful harvest. Nowadays, it is traditional to meet family and friends, picnic beneath the trees and sing songs together. The sakura petals and leaves can be cured and used to flavor ice cream or teas for the celebrations.

The short-lived blossoms symbolize the fragile beauty of life and are central to many folk tales. One story concerns the "Cherry Tree of the Sixteenth Day," an ancient tree that was said to bloom out of season, on the sixteenth day of the first month, when snow still covered the ground.

The story goes that the tree was inhabited by the spirit of a samurai who grew up playing beneath it as a child. Every year, his family decorated the tree with

paper ribbons and praised its beauty, and he taught his children to do the same. But the samurai grew very old and outlived his children, finding himself alone in the world, with the cherry tree his only companion. When the tree died, the man's grief was great and although his neighbors planted a new tree for him, he knew he would never get over his loss. And so he laid out a white sheet on the ground beneath the old tree and begged for it to bloom again, offering his life in return. He committed *hara-kiri,* taking his own life, and his spirit entered the tree, which has blossomed in his memory on the same day ever since - the sixteenth day of the first month.

✶ WEATHER LORE ✶

Plants are nature's calendar, and there are many superstitions relating to trees and the weather:

- **"Oak before ash, we'll have only a splash; ash before oak, we're in for a soak."** Trees coming into leaf are not, unfortunately, a reliable predictor of rain. In fact, a German proverb cites the opposite of this!
- **Pine cones close up when rain is coming.** It's true that pine cones close in humid weather, which can indicate a storm is on its way.
- **If rowan trees bear plenty of fruit, it's a sign of a hard winter to come.** Botanists agree that bountiful berries are the result of a summer free from drought, rather than a sign of weather to come.
- **A persimmon seed can predict the winter ahead.** Although there's no science to back this up, it's fun to cut open the seed and check the pattern inside. A spoon shape means heavy snow, a fork means the snowfall will be lighter and a knife shape means the wind will cut like a blade.

✶ THE JUNIPER TREE ✶

The tree at the center of this traditional German folk tale, retold by the Brothers Grimm, represents new life, although the events surrounding it are grim indeed. The story begins with a couple who long for a child. The woman cuts her finger beneath the juniper tree and, as her blood drips onto the ground, she wishes for a baby. Her wish is granted, but she dies after her son is born and she is buried beneath the tree.

As the boy grows, he is mistreated by his father's new wife. She plots to kill him, succeeds and buries his bones beneath the tree, but a beautiful bird emerges from the branches and flies among the townsfolk, singing a song about the brutal murder. The bird is given a millstone, which it drops on the evil stepmother, killing her. Finally, in a flash of smoke, the bird transforms into the boy, alive and well.

The juniper tree stands out among the darker elements of this tale, symbolizing nature, the circle of life, reincarnation and hope.

✶ SINISTER TREES ✶

Some trees have attracted negative associations over the centuries. Let's take a (cautious!) look at them.

- **Walnut:** Since Roman times, the walnut has been considered a tree of ill omen, perhaps because very few plants can grow beneath it. They're killed off by a toxin called juglone that leaches from the tree. Walnut trees came to be associated with witches, and dreaming of a walnut meant infidelity. In hoodoo tradition, walnuts were used to jinx people.
- **Willow:** Despite its healing qualities, the willow in folklore was considered a sinister tree, capable of uprooting itself and pursuing unsuspecting travelers. It has a long association with sorrow and death. In Belarus, there's a belief that weeping willows are mothers who have lost their children. Mourners traditionally placed willow twigs in coffins and planted saplings on graves to help their loved ones pass into the afterlife.

- **Yew:** Yews are so poisonous that we take our name for poison – "toxin" – from their Latin name: *Taxus baccata.* Perhaps it's not surprising that this tree is associated with death. They're found in churchyards, which were often built on old pagan burial sites, where yews were planted. Sleeping under a yew tree was once believed to cause death. Sprigs of yew were handed out by the ancient Druids at Samhain (now 31 October) to aid communication with loved ones who had passed on.
- **Cypress:** Fragrant cypress wood is used for funeral pyres in India, coffins in Japan, and was used to make chests for mummies in Egypt. Burning it releases a cleansing fungicide into the air, as well as a pleasant scent, so it's easy to see why these trees are regarded as a gateway between life and death. Cut one down at your peril, for you will face grave misfortune if you do.
- **Monkey puzzle:** These trees were thought to be troublesome for humans as well as monkeys – one belief was that the devil lived inside them. Attract his attention when walking past and you will experience bad luck, or even grow a monkey's tail!

✶ TRADITIONAL TREE GAMES 

Conkers is a game using horse chestnuts that has been popular in Britain since the eighteenth century. Tradition has it you should whisper, "Oddly, oddly, onker, my first conker" when you find your first glossy brown seed. In the Torres Strait Islands, the children play *kai*, in which players stand in a circle and hit the deep-red oval fruit of the kai tree with the flat of their hand, keeping the fruit in the air for as long as possible.

Popular in East Africa, *bao* is a fast and furious game where seeds of the msolo tree are exchanged between rows of pits (on a board or dug into the earth). It is a form of *mancala*, a game that dates back 3,500 years, played with the seeds of indigenous trees (oil palm seeds in Cameroon; candlenuts in India; wild orange tree seeds in Kenya). Capturing these seeds represents a ripe fruit for the successful player.

In north-west Queensland, the roots of the white gum tree were used by the Maidhargari children to play *turi turi*, a group skipping game. And throughout North America, Indigenous peoples played lacrosse with sticks made from pliable branches of hickory.

THE WOOD WIDE WEB

The idea that trees are connected by an underground network of fungi, sharing resources and communicating with one another, is relatively new to science. But researchers have recently mapped the wood wide web on a global scale and discovered that around 60 per cent of the world's trees are plugged into it. They can alert their neighbors to danger (emitting signals when predators attack), and send nutrients to neighboring trees – vital for saplings hidden in the shade of more mature companions.

Central to the wood wide web are "hub trees." These are larger, older individuals with more connections and deeper roots, better able to reach and share nutrients. There's some evidence that these "mother trees" can detect distress signals from their companions and help them out accordingly.

In the past, most people considered trees to be individuals at odds with each other, competing for nutrients and light, but perhaps we can learn a little about ourselves when we consider this community of plants quietly co-existing and looking out for one another's needs.

VITS (VERY IMPORTANT TREES)

Trees are the heart of many a folk tale, and some can even claim their place at key moments in history:

- **The Royal Oak:** In 1651, Charles II hid from his parliamentarian pursuers in a grand oak at Boscobel House in Shropshire, England.
- **Isaac Newton's apple tree:** The "gravity tree" is a tourists' favorite in Newton's garden, England.
- **The Emancipation Oak:** In 1861, Mary S. Peake first taught the children of people who had escaped slavery to read and write beneath this sprawling oak. The tree still stands in the grounds of what has become Hampton University, Virginia.
- **The Major Oak:** Another hideaway, this giant in Sherwood Forest, England, is said to have concealed Robin Hood and his Merry Men in its branches.
- **The Liberty Tree:** This powerful symbol of patriotism was an old elm in Boston, decorated with banners by protestors in 1765.

✶ TREES OF LOVE ✶

In the days before dating apps, the ash tree was your best option when looking for love. A woman carrying an ash leaf could be sure that the first man she saw would be her future husband. A marginally less risky tradition, at Christmas gatherings, was to burn a bundle of ash poles bound with flexible stems of ash. Unmarried folk could each choose a bundle and, if the band around theirs burst into flames first, they would be the next to marry.

Thanks to its association with the Greek goddess Aphrodite, the apple tree is also known as a tree of love. In Poland, a young woman putting an apple under her pillow on New Year's Eve would dream of her future husband, or she might prefer peeling an apple while looking in a mirror. (Throwing the peel over her shoulder would reveal her true love's initial!) Apple blossom can be used in love spells, and if you want your deepest wish to come true, just whisper it into a ribbon and tie it to the branch of an apple tree.

✶ THE TALE OF ASH LAD ✶

The tree in this Swedish folk tale isn't an ash, it's a mighty oak that grew outside the king's window and couldn't be chopped down. So annoyed was the king with this tree that he decreed whoever could rid him of it would win his daughter's hand in marriage. News of this reached three brothers living nearby, and the eldest decided to try his luck. He took with him his youngest brother, who was named Ash Lad because he spent most of his time staring into the ashes of the fire.

On the way, Ash Lad found an enchanted axe chopping a tree by itself. "Pick me up," the axe said, "and things will go well for you." Ash Lad did so. When they arrived at the palace, his brother tried to cut down the tree, using his own axe, but failed. The tree only grew bigger. They gave up and went home.

Next, the second brother took up the challenge, and Ash Lad went with him, finding an enchanted spade, digging by itself, on the way. "Take me with you," said the spade, "and you won't be disappointed." Ash Lad did so. At the palace, his brother chopped at the tree, but his efforts only made it larger. He, too, gave up and they returned home.

Finally, Ash Lad decided to tackle the tree. On his way to the palace, he came to a river. "Follow me to my source," it said, "and you will be glad you did." Ash Lad followed the river and saw that its waters were flowing from a hole in the side of a hazelnut. He put a plug in the hole, took the nut and carried on to the palace, where he used his enchanted axe to tackle the oak. The axe cut through the trunk like a knife through cheese, and the mighty tree fell.

But before he could claim the princess's hand, the king challenged Ash Lad to dig a well and fill it with water. Swiftly he set the spade to work digging a hole. Next he took the nut, removed the plug and let the water fill the well. Astonished, the king embraced Ash Lad and welcomed him as his new son-in-law.

CHAPTER TWO:
TREES IN MYTHOLOGY

We've discovered some fascinating tree folklore and tales - the wisdom and stories of everyday life passed down from our forebears - but now let's travel farther back in time and explore ancient stories of mythical beasts, gods battling mortals, and the creation of the planet itself...

Trees had already existed for millions of years when humans were taking their first tentative steps beneath them, so it's no wonder that they appear in our creation myths and the stories of our oldest civilizations. In these tales, trees take on a sacred role - symbolizing life, wisdom and the connection between the human realm and the divine - and we'll travel from the classical worlds of ancient Rome and Greece to Mexico, Japan and South America to uncover them. We'll meet the weird and wonderful creatures that live in the mighty Yggdrasil; the three-legged crows that call the Fusang tree home; and the peculiar fruit of the Jinmenju tree. We'll discover trees that grant wishes, trees that become human, humans that become trees and a gruesome vampiric tree found only on battlefields.

✶ THE WORLD TREE ✶

The World Tree is a central motif in myths from around the globe; it's usually depicted as a mighty tree (the species varies) that bridges the gap between heaven and earth, with its roots extending down into the underworld. The trunk represents the middle realm, the world of mankind. Gods and other higher beings live at the top of the tree, while below ground the roots are home to a variety of malevolent creatures.

In China, the tree is called Jianmu, but climb it at your peril, for if you look down while you make your ascent, you will come crashing back to earth. Hungarian myth describes the *égig érő fa* (sky-high tree), that only shamans may climb to reach enlightenment. In Mayan culture, the tree trunk was sometimes represented as a caiman, while in northern Germany the tree was thought to have iron roots, copper branches and silver leaves. Perhaps the most well-known example of the World Tree, though, comes from Norse mythology. It is Yggdrasil, the mighty ash (see page 42).

THE FLOOD MYTH OF THE HUICHOL

The Huichol are an Indigenous people who live in the Sierra Madre Occidental region. They have a flood myth that evolved quite separately from Christian tales of Noah and his ark, and many versions of their story begin with trees.

Every morning Watákame and his little black dog would head out to sow corn, chopping down trees to clear space as they went. Yet, overnight, the trees would mysteriously grow back. One night, Watákame kept watch to see what was happening, and found that an elderly woman was responsible – he discovered she was Nakawé, the goddess of living things.

Nakawé warned Watákame that a great deluge was coming and that the only way to survive was to carve a canoe from the largest tree he could find. He must set the canoe on top of the highest mountain, and take with him seeds and plants, fire and, of course, his dog. Watákame did as he was bid and survived the flood, becoming the father of the Huichol people in the New World that emerged.

IN THE BEGINNING...

It is easy to see how trees - with their longevity and seemingly magickal ability to shed and regrow their leaves - have come to play a part in the creation myths of many cultures. In Norse mythology, the first man and woman (Ask and Embla) were formed from a fallen ash and a fallen elm, brought to life by the gods. A similar thing happens in a Passamaquoddy creation legend, although the first men were drawn from ash trees when the creator fired an arrow into their bark. Meanwhile, in Zoroastrian myth, a tree is said to have grown from the corpse of the first being, who was neither male nor female. This tree's trunk then separated into two branches, which became the first man and woman, Mashya and Mashyana.

In other creation myths, trees are important in the formation of the earth itself. Iroquois legend describes a woman, one of the Sky People who lived in the Great Blue, who had a premonition that in their realm would grow a large tree, covered in white blossoms that would bring light to the world when opened, but bring darkness when they closed. When her prediction came true, the Sky People wanted to remove the tree and dug

a hole around its roots. It fell through the hole into the sea below, leaving them in darkness. The Sky People blamed the woman and sent her down after the tree, where she was aided by various sea animals to create the land.

The Christian story of the Garden of Eden involves two trees - the Tree of Life and the Tree of Knowledge - and Micronesian myth offers us a story with some interesting similarities. The first humans lived in a garden, watched over by their creator, Na Kaa. They gathered under two trees: the men under one, and the women under the other. Na Kaa warned them not to stray from these places, but one day, when he was away, they mingled together under a different tree. When Na Kaa returned, he told them they'd chosen the Tree of Death, and so humans became mortal.

✶ THE WISH-GRANTING TREE ✶

Hindus know the World Tree as Kalpavriksha, and it is said that it will grant a wish to those who stand beneath it. The tree was created during the "churning of the ocean milk," part of the ongoing battle between gods and demons, and many other treasures emerged from the ocean at the same time, including the sacred cow of plenty and *amrita*, the elixir of immortality. Lord Indra took the tree to heaven, away from any who would misuse its power by wishing for evil things.

In some versions of the story of Kalpavriksha, Parvati, the mother goddess, filled with loneliness after the loss of her son, asked her husband, Shiva, to take her to the garden where Kalpavriksha was found. Beneath the tree she wished for a daughter, and her wish was granted. Another tale describes Parvati and Shiva giving away their daughter, Aranyani, to the tree for safekeeping during a time of war against the demon Andhakasura. She became the goddess of forests and wild animals.

WHAT DO TREES DO FOR ME?

If the idea of trees granting wishes or giving humans life seems fanciful, take a look at this list of the amazing services that trees provide and think again. Of course, we should value trees as fellow living beings – not simply as a resource – but reminding ourselves of their vital role can help us appreciate how important it is to protect them. Trees...

- Clean the air, removing carbon dioxide (which causes global heating) and replacing it with oxygen
- Store carbon within themselves, removing it from the atmosphere
- Boost our immune systems
- Provide food and habitat for thousands of species
- Protect the soil and prevent it from being washed away
- Cool the atmosphere and add moisture via evaporation
- Add biodiversity to benefit future generations
- Reduce pollution in affected areas by up to 50 per cent

HERACLES AND THE GOLDEN APPLES

When Hera and Zeus married, they were gifted a sacred apple tree, which Hera planted at the center of her orchard. The tree bore golden fruit, and King Eurystheus decreed that, for his eleventh labor, Heracles (later known as Hercules) must steal three of them. This was no easy task, as the location of the tree was a secret, and it was guarded by nine maidens (the Hesperides) and a serpent, Ladon, that never slept.

The Old Man of the Sea directed Heracles to the tree and advised him not to pick the fruit himself, but to ask Atlas, father of the Hesperides, to do it for him. Atlas agreed to fetch the apples, but only if Heracles killed Ladon and took over Atlas's burden, bearing the globe on his back. Heracles agreed, but knew the Titan would try to trick him into carrying the globe permanently. Once he'd picked the apples, Atlas refused to take back the sphere, but Heracles tricked him into holding it "while he adjusted his cloak" and made off with the fruit instead.

THE LADY OF THE SYCAMORE

Trees in ancient Egypt were few and far between, a precious commodity indeed. Many of them were linked with gods. Thoth and Seshat, the deities associated with words and writing, would inscribe the length of a pharaoh's reign on the leaves of the ished tree, for example, while Ra, the sun god, was associated with the sycamore tree. The *Book of the Dead* describes two turquoise sycamores growing at the point on the horizon where Ra would rise every morning.

The tree in question is *Ficus sycomorus*, the sycamore fig, which grows along riverbanks and produces fruit throughout the year. The fruit - a staple in the ancient Egyptian diet - was often paired with wine in celebrations, particularly those associated with Hathor, who was goddess of music, dance and the dead. She was known as the "Lady of the Sycamore" and was often depicted walking through groves of sycamore, offering fresh water to the spirits of the deceased who hung from their branches.

✶ YGGDRASIL ✶

Norse legend tells us that Yggdrasil stands at the center of the cosmos, its roots and branches binding together the nine worlds around it, and beneath this mighty ash the gods hold their daily courts. The tree's name means "Horse of Odin," for it is here, they say, that the All-Father sacrificed himself, flinging himself upon his sword and hanging in the tree's branches to gain enlightenment. He remained suspended upside-down for nine days and nights, during which he had many visions. The knowledge Odin gained, which he passed on through the runes, was said to include how to cure the sick, calm storms, and disarm his attackers, as well as make women fall in love.

The tree's large roots were thought to lead to different regions of the earth. One version of the myth describes three roots: one leading to Hel's realm of the dead; another to the icy world of the frost giants; and the third to Midgard, where humankind resides. The Well of Mimir, a source of wisdom, was also found beneath the tree, and Odin left an eye here in exchange for the insight and understanding he gained drinking from its waters. Alongside this was the Well of

Fate, home to three giantesses, the Norns, who drew its water to nourish Yggdrasil.

The tree was also home to four stags, who lived among its branches, browsing from the leafy canopy, along with a mighty dragon, Níðhöggr, who tore at its roots. (This nibbling away of the tree represents the mortality of the cosmos.) On top of the tree lived an eagle, who represented wisdom and foresight, and who exchanged insults with the dragon at its roots via Ratatöskr, a squirrel who scurried up and down the trunk between their two realms.

THE TREE OF THE TEN SUNS

An ancient Chinese myth describes the sacred Fusang tree, a tree of tremendous height (perhaps a mulberry) that grew on an island in the east, where the sun rises. Ten suns could be found in the branches of the Fusang tree, although only one of them would journey across the sky each day. Some versions of the tale describe a matching tree in the west, Ruomu, and say that the sun would set there.

As with many legends, there are different versions of the story. Some sources tell us that the sun was carried across the sky by one of ten three-legged sun crows. Every day a different sun crow would carry the sun across the heavens while the other nine rested in the tree. Later versions of the story describe the enormous red fruits of the Fusang tree, which only appeared every 9,000 years but had the power to turn golden anyone who ate them.

THE SALMON OF KNOWLEDGE

To the Celts, hazelnuts symbolized wisdom, and this story tells us how Ffion Mac Cumhail came to inherit all the wisdom of the world.

Once there was a sacred pool around which nine hazelnut trees grew. Whenever a hazelnut fell into the water, the large salmon living there would eat the nut and absorb its wisdom. It was said that whoever ate the salmon would become the wisest person alive, and Finegas – a poet – was determined he would be the one to catch it. Finegas spent years fishing for the salmon until one day he finally spotted it. He struggled to land his catch and then asked Ffion, the young warrior he was teaching, to cook the salmon for him, warning him not to eat any of the flesh. As Ffion was turning the salmon over the fire, a drop of fish-oil burned his thumb and he sucked it to stop the pain. Finegas soon realized Ffion had tasted the salmon's wisdom and encouraged him to eat the whole fish, gaining the knowledge to be the wisest leader of the Fianna warriors.

TREE TRANSFORMATIONS

Many creation stories tell us about trees becoming the first people, but there are plenty of other myths, particularly from classical sources, about humans being turned into trees.

DAPHNE BECOMES A LAUREL TREE

Tired of running from speedy Apollo, and uninterested in his advances, the beautiful nymph Daphne called to her father, the river god Peneus, for help. He turned her into a laurel tree. Apollo's association with the laurel and the Olympics led to the crowning of victors with laurel wreaths and to the use of the word "laureate" to mean the esteemed winner of an award.

THE SEVEN POPLARS

The sun god Helios had seven nymph daughters, the Heliades. When their brother, Phaethon, begged his father to let him drive the sun's chariot across the sky, he lost control and crashed into the earth, setting the lands of Africa ablaze. Zeus was so furious at this carelessness that he struck the boy down and the Heliades gathered to mourn him on the banks of the Eridanos. Their grief

was so great that they were transformed into poplars and their tears into amber.

LOTIS'S METAMORPHOSIS

Another nymph forced to turn into a tree to escape unwanted advances, Lotis was disturbed while resting under a tree by the lecherous Priapus. A braying donkey stopped him in his tracks and Lotis found sanctuary when she was transformed into a lotus tree.

BAUCIS AND PHILEMON

When this elderly couple welcomed two strangers into their home during a terrible storm and shared with them their few supplies, they were rewarded with two wishes, for the visitors were none other than Zeus and Hermes in disguise. The couple wished for a temple where they might worship the gods, and also to die together so that neither should ever be without the other. The gods granted their wishes, and when the pair died, they were transformed into an oak and a linden tree with their branches forever entwined.

✶ THE MUURBAY TREE ✶

The story holders of the Gumbaynggirr people tell this tale of the Muurbay tree from long ago. The Muurbay was an enormous white fig; so large, it was said, that it covered around an acre of land. The tree was the source of food for the entire tribe, and people would come from far and wide to gather around it when the time came for the sacred fruit to be picked. They would celebrate and exchange stories together, but one day they began to argue about who had a right to pick the fruit and how that fruit was shared.

When the Father, Baabaga, heard the people's angry words, he pulled up the tree as a punishment. And though the people pulled on the tree's roots, they couldn't stop him from taking the Muurbay up into the sky. Since then, whenever a member of the Gumbaynggirr tribe dies, it is said that their spirit stops at the Muurbay tree to eat its fruit before they journey on.

RECORD-BREAKING TREES

Awe-inspiring trees don't just exist in ancient myths; there are some pretty impressive specimens out there in the real world, too. Here are just a few:

- **Hyperion:** This giant redwood, found in California, is the tallest tree on the planet. At 116 metres (381 feet), it's taller than the Statue of Liberty.
- **Pando:** This colony of 47,000 genetically identical aspens is actually the world's largest tree. Pando has been growing in Utah for 80,000 years and is the world's heaviest living organism.
- **The oldest individual trees:** Several bristlecone pines have been dated as over 4,500 years old, including Methuselah, in California's Inyo County. However, yew trees can also be very long-living, and the Fortingall Yew in Scotland has been assessed as around 5,000 years old.
- **The earliest surviving species of tree** is the *Ginkgo biloba* (maidenhair tree) from Zhejiang in China. Fossils from this tree have been found dating to around 160 million years ago.

OSIRIS AND THE WILLOW TREE

It is said that before Osiris became the god of the underworld, he ruled Egypt as its first king, alongside his queen and sister, Isis. His success was so great that his brother Seth plotted to kill Osiris and take his place. To carry out his plan, Seth organized a feast and invited all the great and the good to attend. The centerpiece of his celebration was a magnificent chest, fashioned from willow, and admired by all. Seth announced that whoever fitted into the chest would be able to keep it. One by one, the guests took their turn to lie in the chest, unaware that Seth had made it the perfect size for one person only: Osiris. When Osiris tried the chest for size, Seth hurriedly closed the lid and fastened it tight before casting it into the River Nile. The chest had become Osiris's coffin.

The coffin eventually came to shore at Byblos, where a willow tree grew up around it, concealing it entirely. The tree was cut down to be used in building the palace of King Byblos, but Isis felt the power emanating from the tree and came in disguise in search of her husband. She was able to retrieve the chest, but when she opened

it, Osiris was dead. Seth, furious to learn that his brother had been discovered, cut his corpse into fourteen pieces and buried them throughout Egypt. Isis was able to retrieve all of them except his penis, which had been eaten by a fish in the Nile. She was able to resurrect her husband, but he was sent to rule the underworld.

The doomed king's connection with willow trees could be seen in the many towns in Egypt that were believed to have been the burial sites of parts of his corpse. All of them had willow groves, and many would enact a festival called Raising the Willow every year to ensure the continued fertility of their plants and trees.

✶ MYTHICAL OLIVES ✶

Olive trees are as central to classical myths as they were to life centuries ago. Wild olives existed around 7,000 years ago, but legend has it that Athena created the first olive tree in Athens. Athena and Poseidon were competing to offer the most precious gift to humanity in return for the honor of naming the city. Poseidon created the horse, offering the people a speedy advantage in battle. Athena, meanwhile, created the olive tree to give people fuel and nourishment. Zeus judged Athena's gift the most peaceful and valuable, and so the competition was won. Because of this association, the tree was considered sacred and anyone who dared to harm it would be severely punished.

The olive crops up in both the *Iliad* and the *Odyssey*: Odysseus blinds the Cyclops with a pointed olive stake heated in a fire. And - aside from his 12 labors - Heracles was said to have used an olive club formed from a tree he tore up on Mount Helicon to defeat the Lion of Cithaeron. It seems olive trees weren't always used for peaceful purposes!

JUBOKKO AND JINMENJU 

Japanese myth offers us two types of tree that have a rather creepy connection to humans. The first is the Jubokko – also known as the vampire tree, as it was said to grow on battlefields where many casualties have fallen, living on the blood they left behind. Jubokko trees had a gruesome ability: to shape their branches into tubes and suck the blood out of unsuspecting people passing by.

The second type of tree is known as the Jinmenju (or Ninmenju), which, it is said, produces fruit that look like human heads. Although the heads cannot speak, they can laugh, but if they laugh too much the fruit will fall to the ground. The Jinmenju legend is thought to have originated in China, and similar stories of trees bearing human fruit can be found in Indian and Persian myth.

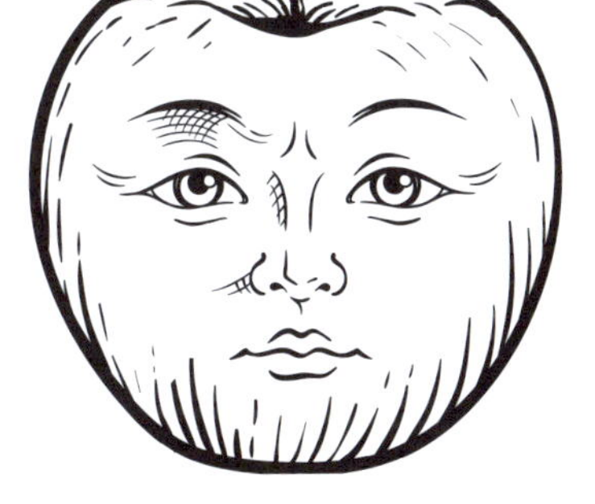

THE TREES OF ANCIENT ROME

- **Groves of trees** were considered sacred in Rome and were sites of worship, with Romans distinguishing between a *lucus* (a group of sacred trees in the wild) and a *nemus* (a series of well-ordered, planted trees). Venus was the goddess of fertility (among other things) and her temples would often be situated near a grove of trees.
- The **holly tree** was the sacred tree of Saturn, which is why Roman households decorated their homes with holly branches during the winter festival of Saturnalia – a week of partying and gambling in which masters would serve their slaves and gifts of holly were exchanged.
- **Oak trees** were revered for their connection with Jupiter and symbolized virtue, strength and courage. Oak-leaf coronets were awarded to victorious Roman commanders, while the *corona civica*, a civilian award, was an oak-leaf crown given to citizens who had saved the lives of others.

- When the mythical founders of Rome, Romulus and Remus, were abandoned and left floating in a cradle down the Tiber, it was under a **fig tree** that they came to rest. The twins were suckled by a she-wolf in the shade of the tree and this *Ficus ruminalis* was highly significant in ancient Roman culture. A fig tree grew in the Forum, as a symbolic reminder of the *Ficus ruminalis*; if the tree ever shriveled up, it was thought to be a bad omen and priests hurried to replace it.
- **Myrtle** was considered a symbol of good luck, and people might wear a wreath of myrtle when setting off on their travels. In the Aeneid, when Aeneas tries to uproot a bush of myrtle to use the branches to protect an altar, the ground begins to bleed and Aeneas hears the voice of Polydorus, a murder victim who has been buried in that very spot. It was also said that a pair of myrtle trees grew outside one of Rome's most ancient temples: one would flourish when the senate was at its most powerful, the other when the plebeians' power was dominant.

CHAPTER THREE:

TREES AS SYMBOLS

Trees are powerful symbols: thanks to their size and longevity, their ability to renew themselves with the turning of the seasons and their network of roots and branches, they have come to represent everything from life and death to wisdom and growth. With over 10,000 years of tree symbolism, this is a rich vein for us to explore.

After many years of research, investigating how often people dreamed of trees, psychologist Carl Jung concluded that trees are an archetype – a symbol so relevant to the human experience that it is stored in the subconscious of people the world over. In dreams, he said, they represent growth, development, safety, shelter, nourishment, death and rebirth.

Because of this, trees are relevant in most cultures and religious traditions, and this chapter covers everything from their role in ancient scripture and pagan ritual to their symbolism in art and society today. We'll also meet some inspirational trees surviving against the odds and discover a tree so revered that it has its own security team.

TREES IN ISLAM

A significant tree in Islam is known as the Lote Tree of the Utmost Boundary. The Qur'an tells Muslims that this tree marks the point beyond which humans and angels cannot pass on their journey toward God, and so it represents the limit of human understanding. Muhammad is said to have passed beyond this tree to receive God's wisdom and knowledge of the five daily prayers.

Other trees mentioned in the Qur'an - as with many holy scriptures - reflect the species that were important to people hundreds of years ago, since they were used for food or fuel. There are references to the date palm, for example, whose fruits are symbolic of the good deeds that strengthen faith, and the olive tree, which represents purity. Olive oil was burned in lamps and symbolizes the light of Allah in the Qur'an.

A central tenet in Islam is preserving life, and planting trees is seen as an act of *Sadaqah Jariyah* (continuing charity). It is something that practicing Muslims may carry out at any time of year, but particularly during Ramadan.

✶ THE TREE OF LIFE ✶

The Tree of Life is a potent symbol: a mature tree with a sturdy trunk and widely spreading roots and branches, it represents growth, connection and the cyclical nature of life. Its roots burrow deep into the earth, symbolizing grounding and the past, while its branches stretch toward the sky, representing aspirations, future growth and the divine.

Closely connected to the concept of the World Tree (see page 34), the Tree of Life is significant in many religions, where its fruit often represent spiritual nourishment, or the results of our actions. In some religions, it can signify eternal life: in the Bible, it is found in the Garden of Eden, while the Qur'an mentions the Tree of Eternity. The oldest example of the symbol itself was found on Mesopotamian burial vessels from 7000 BCE, but 9,000 years later it is still as powerful and relevant, offering us harmony, balance and a timeless link to the cosmos and our place within it.

AGAINST THE ODDS

Nothing symbolizes the power of nature quite like a lone tree growing where it has no business to be. The trees on this page are bold survivors, flourishing against the odds, and perhaps they resonate with us on a deeper level, too. It's difficult not to feel sorry for these lonely souls, cut off from their companions.

- **The Ranfurly Tree:** Planted in 1901 by Lord Ranfurly, this Sitka spruce on New Zealand's Campbell Island holds the world record for the planet's remotest tree: there isn't another for 222 kilometres (138 miles). The spruce is not native to its Antarctic location, but despite facing wild winds and 325 days of rain a year, it is flourishing.
- **Fred the Tree:** The sight of this Australian pine on the old Seven Mile Bridge that connects Florida Keys to the US mainland is as incongruous as it is inspiring. It's believed Fred came to make his home on this narrow strip of concrete surrounded by sparkling ocean when he seeded from bird droppings about 30 years ago. Fred has become a symbol of the resilience of the Florida Keys folk,

having survived several hurricanes, and is something of a celebrity, appearing on souvenirs and having his own Facebook page.

- **The Tree of Ténéré:** A former holder of the "Remotest Tree" title, this acacia in Niger was the only tree for 400 kilometres (249 miles). A Saharan landmark, featured on local maps, it had deep roots that tapped into a nearby well. Sadly, the 300-year-old tree was knocked down and destroyed by a truck driver in the 1970s.
- **Moon trees:** Although the sycamores, redwoods and fir trees on NASA's list of "moon trees" are growing in traditional locations across the US and beyond, they have a very unusual provenance. These special individuals have been grown from seeds that went into orbit around the moon with NASA astronaut Stuart Roosa on the *Apollo 14* mission in 1971. Not only did many of the seeds survive their space adventure, they also survived an accidental spillage during decontamination when the crew returned to earth.

✶ ANCIENT WISDOM ✶

It's easy to see why trees symbolize ancient wisdom. They can live for hundreds of years – long enough to witness the land and its people change around them, and to gain the insight of the old.

Beech trees have always had a particularly close connection with knowledge. The first "book" was formed when words were written on slivers of beech wood, and this link between the beech tree and the written word has been captured in language itself. *Boc* was Anglo-Saxon for "beech," and in many languages the word for "book" is a close match.

In ancient times, anyone who had power over the written word was considered mighty indeed, such as the Irish warrior Ogma. Ogma was credited with inventing the Ogham alphabet (see page 71), which was named after him. This system, in use by Celtic peoples from the fourth century CE, comprises 20 symbols, which are believed to represent particular trees and their attributes. It has been developed today for use in divination, as a way to tap into the ancient wisdom of trees.

THE SURVIVOR TREE

Trees are known for their resilience; some species are able to withstand wild weather, salty water or extremes of temperature. But the discovery of a battered and broken Callery pear tree beneath the rubble at Ground Zero several weeks after the 9/11 attacks astonished everyone: one branch of the badly burned tree was still alive. The tree was carefully removed to a nursery in the Bronx, where it showed signs of recovery. It was nurtured, survived being uprooted in a storm, and was finally returned to the World Trade Center site in 2010, where it forms a key part of the memorial plaza, standing as a symbol of resilience, survival and rebirth.

The tree has gone on to spread its message of hope around the world as, every year since 2013, three of its seedlings have been sent to communities across the world who have also lost citizens to tragedies and have promised to nurture the seedling in their memory. Many of these "survivor trees" now stand at the center of memorials of their own.

THE KABBALISTIC TREE OF LIFE

The idea of a tree of life with spheres representing spiritual nodes has roots in early Assyrian culture, but the traditional diagram used in Kabbalah originated in the early thirteenth century. It represents the flow of energy from the infinite source above to finite manifestation below, and symbolizes the way the universe came into being. Ten spiritual concepts (known as sephirot) are shown in the spheres, laid out in three columns, with 22 pathways linking them. Divine energy enters at the Crown (Kether) and flows through to Malkuth at the root, symbolizing grounding and manifestation.

The Kabbalistic Tree of Life can be used as a tool to understand the way things manifest in our lives, and – with the sephirot representing energy centers in the body – can be used in meditation. If we look at the arrangement of sephirot in three horizontal triads, we can see them as representing intellect, emotion and instinct, while the three columns, Kabbalists say, show that our path through life should be one of balance, where we must experience the polarities and find a harmonious route through them.

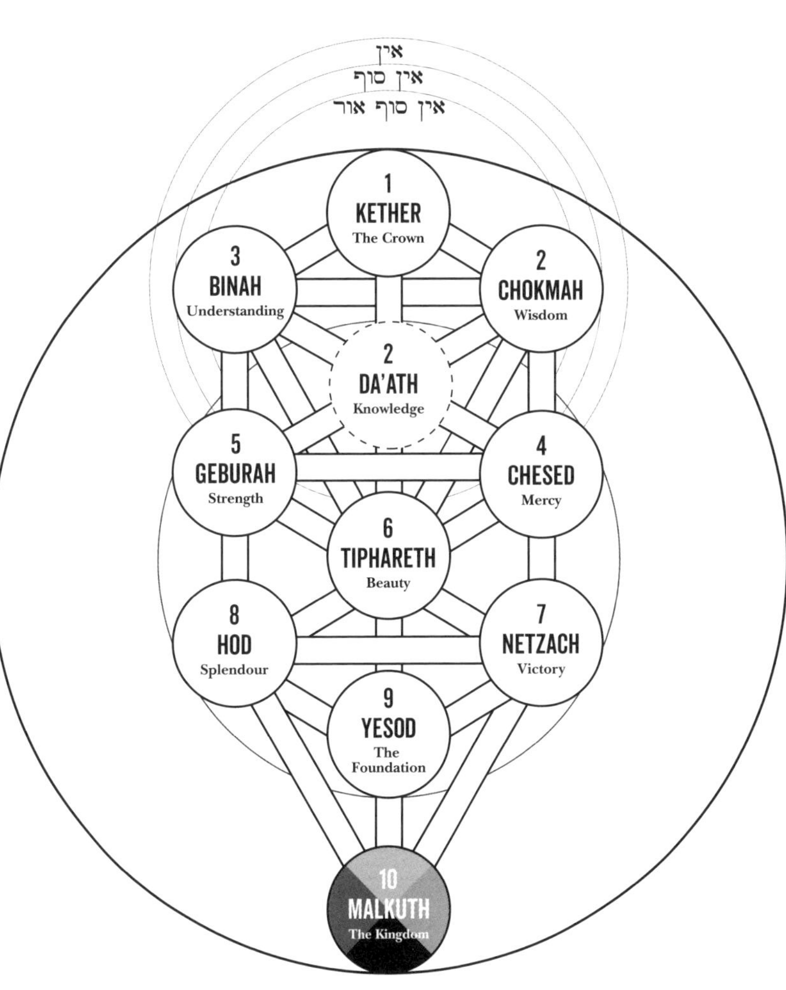
אין
אין סוף
אין סוף אור
1
KETHER
The Crown
3
BINAH
Understanding
2
CHOKMAH
Wisdom
2
DA'ATH
Knowledge
5
GEBURAH
Strength
4
CHESED
Mercy
6
TIPHARETH
Beauty
8
HOD
Splendour
7
NETZACH
Victory
9
YESOD
The
Foundation
10
MALKUTH
The Kingdom

MIRACULOUS MANGROVES AND OTHER ADAPTATIONS

Like many wonders of nature, trees have adapted to best survive their environment and maximize their access to the resources they need. The average oak, for example, has 250,000 leaves, every one providing a surface for gas exchange (absorbing carbon dioxide and emitting oxygen) and filled with chlorophyll for photosynthesis (the process plants use to turn light energy into sugars).

Some trees have adapted to survive in areas other plants would find inhospitable, such as wildfire zones. The lodgepole pine has cones sealed with a resin that melts when exposed to the heat of a fire, triggering the growth of seedlings. Giant sequoias have thick, fire-retardant bark, and some eucalyptus trees have buds waiting to regrow beneath their bark if it is burned away.

Mangrove trees, meanwhile, have some amazing adaptations that allow them to survive in the salt-water conditions of tropical and sub-tropical areas. There are over 50 species of these hugely important trees, which act as barriers protecting the land during extreme

weather, provide habitat for marine life and a nursery for juvenile fish, and together absorb around four times as much carbon as rainforests. Some survive the high salinity levels of the ocean water by excreting salt through special salt glands on their leaves. Salt crystals build up on the leaves, which eventually fall off, taking the salt with them.

The trees' roots are specially adapted, too. Some have strong buttress roots to support them against incoming tides, while others have "knee roots" that grow out horizontally from the trunk and then descend into the water. The exposed part of the root has pores to absorb oxygen. Other species have pneumatophores, snorkel-like roots that extend up out of the ground, allowing them to absorb oxygen when their base is submerged.

Mangroves have even adapted the way they reproduce to take advantage of their watery environment. Once pollinated, mangrove seedlings start growing while still attached to the parent tree. They are then released into the water, float away and eventually sink into the soil to take root a safe distance from their parent, to avoid competing with them for resources.

✶ THE GREEN MAN ✶

You might spot him looking down impassively from the stonework of a church or smiling enigmatically from a pub sign: the face of a man with leaves in place of hair and foliage trailing from his mouth. The Green Man is so ancient that he has become more of an archetype than a symbol. This fusion of man and plant represents fertility, masculinity, and rebirth and crops up in various guises. We meet him as Puck, John Barleycorn (a symbol of the autumn harvest), or Jack in the Green (a jester-like figure at Beltane celebrations).

Perhaps it's no surprise that today, with nature facing greater challenges than ever, this ancient symbol representing life on earth – this guardian of our forests – is experiencing such a resurgence in popularity.

✦ PLANTING TREES ✦

The fact that trees will be here when we're long gone - and were here long before we arrived, too - makes planting a tree such a meaningful act. We may do it to commemorate an anniversary, to mark the site of an event or, on a personal level, to remember a loved one. One beautiful example is Whipsnade Tree Cathedral in Bedfordshire, UK. The entire "cathedral," planted in trees and shrubs, was created by Edmund Blyth, who served as an infantryman in World War One and wanted to leave a fitting natural memorial to the friends he lost.

In Jewish tradition, tree-planting may take place as a way of celebrating Tu B'Shevat. This festival is the annual birthday for trees - one of four Jewish New Years - and people traditionally eat fruits mentioned in the Torah, such as figs, pomegranates, olives and dates. They might try a new fruit, too. Fruit trees are given particular reverence in the Torah, as fruit is seen as symbolic of God's favor and gift of life.

THE BODHI TREE

Buddhist tradition describes how Siddhartha Gautama attained enlightenment by meditating under a fig tree in Bodh Gaya, north-eastern India. After seven weeks, he thanked the tree for its shade and left that place having achieved a state of perfect knowledge, becoming the Buddha. The fig tree standing today in the square at Bodh Gaya is a descendant of the original tree, and several other sacred Bodhi trees are believed to have grown from cuttings of the original.

A symbol of spiritual awakening to Buddhists, the sacred fig - *Ficus religiosa* - is also considered significant in Sikhism, Hinduism and Jainism. It symbolizes wisdom and the eternal nature of the soul, and the trees are often used as a site for meditation, a place to seek shade and enlightenment.

✴ THE OGHAM ALPHABET ✴

Trees were central to life in pre-Christian Ireland, where the Ogham alphabet originated; there are over 10,000 places in Ireland that are named after trees. Every clan had their clan tree, or *bile*, under which their chieftain received their title, along with a rod of the sacred wood as a symbol of their leadership.

The origins of the Ogham alphabet are attributed to the warrior Ogma and there are several theories about what these medieval letters mean. It was in use by the fourth century CE and most of the letters are linked to the Celtic words for different trees. The ancient Celts worshipped, observed and understood trees and their various attributes. The tree Ogham developed as a way of combining the Ogham runes with this knowledge, to use the symbols in spell work and meditation if so desired. (Turn to page 118 to find out how to make a set of your own Ogham runes.)

So, what are the 20 different trees, and what do they symbolize? Some common correspondences are listed overleaf.

THE OGHAM TREES AND THEIR MEANINGS

Tree	Gaelic name	Meaning
Birch	*Beith*	New beginnings, fertility
Rowan	*Luis*	Protection, insight
Alder	*Fearn*	Healing, sensitivity
Willow	*Saille*	Friendship, creativity
Ash	*Nuin*	Vision, resilience
Hawthorn	*Huathe*	Challenges
Oak	*Duir*	Strength, wealth
Holly	*Tinne*	Courage
Hazel	*Coll*	Intuition, inspiration

Tree	Gaelic name	Meaning
Apple	*Quert*	Beauty, love, choices
Vine	*Muin*	Prophecy, service
Ivy	*Gort*	The self, patience, trust
Reed	*Ngeadal*	Transformation
Blackthorn	*Straif*	Challenges, ingenuity
Elder	*Ruis*	Healing and releasing the past
Pine	*Ailim*	Far-sightedness, prosperity
Gorse	*Ohn*	Consistency, success
Heather	*Ur*	Healing, inner self
White poplar	*Eadha*	Tension, decisions
Yew	*Ioho*	Letting go, rebirth

THE THREE FRIENDS OF WINTER

Pine, bamboo and plum: these three trees bring color and hope to the otherwise bare branches of winter and so are celebrated together in Chinese culture. Their popularity spread to Japan, where they bring a festive feel to greeting cards celebrating the New Year - and the motif appears in Vietnamese and Korean culture, too. Together the "Three Friends" represent stoicism and perseverance, and Confucianists see these as the ideal characteristics of a scholar and gentleman.

The individual trees also have specific symbolism. Pine, with its evergreen needles that often grow in pairs, represents longevity and, when depicted with the crane, a successful marriage. The hollow trunks of bamboo are so strong they are often used in place of steel girders in construction, so it's easy to see why the tree represents steadfastness. Daoists use bamboo as an example of the principle of inaction. While winds rage around it, the tree bends but does not break - a staunch survivor of challenging times. Meanwhile, the plum tree brings delicate blossom to the late winter and is considered a lucky charm to ward off evil spirits.

THE GUEST-GREETING PINE 

One particular pine tree - atop Huangshan mountain in Anhui province, China - has become such a popular symbol of welcome that it attracts several million visitors a year and has been appointed its very own team of tree guardians. The Guest-Greeting Pine, or *Yingkesong* in Mandarin, has been seen as a symbol of hospitality since the 1950s, thanks to its shape: its long, forked branch extends outwards as if to greet visitors. A metal sculpture of the tree welcomes delegates to the Great Hall of the People, on Tiananmen Square, Beijing, China.

The pine is checked thoroughly every two hours by one of its guardians, who are aided by an intruder-warning system and use everything from a drone to a magnifying glass to ensure the tree is free of damage from animals, tourists and disease. The post requires a year-long apprenticeship during which a new guard not only learns the ropes of the role but also builds up a relationship with this iconic tree.

✶ BIBLICAL TREES ✶

Apart from the Tree of Life and the Tree of Knowledge of Good and Evil, there are 22 species of trees mentioned in the Bible, all of which would have been useful and familiar trees at the time these tales originated. They are the symbolic heart of some allegories, such as "The Parable of the Barren Fig Tree," and key elements in other Bible stories.

- **Olive tree:** With its deep roots and ability to thrive in desert conditions, the olive is symbolic of faith, beauty and abundance. The olive branch - brought back to Noah on the ark by a dove - represents hope and is a universal sign of peace. Two olive branches surround a map of the world on the flag of the United Nations.
- **Palm tree:** Palm trees have symbolized victory since ancient times - victorious Romans might wear a toga decorated with palm leaves - and so waving palm branches to celebrate Jesus's return to Jerusalem was a significant message from his supporters. Today, Christians celebrate this on Palm Sunday, with a procession or with blessed branches or small crosses made from palm fronds or twigs.

- **Judas tree:** Another tree with a Biblical connection, it is said to be so named because Judas Iscariot hanged himself from this tree, having betrayed Jesus. The type of tree was never specified in the Bible, however, and it is much more likely that the tree was originally named after the area where it was found: Judea.
- **Zacchaeus's tree:** Here, the sycamore fig tree plays a central part in the story of Zacchaeus, the tax collector. Unable to see over the crowds, Zacchaeus climbs the tree to get a glimpse of Jesus and is rewarded with a visit from him, much to the dismay of the rest of the gathered throng.

CHAPTER FOUR:

TREE WORSHIP AND DEITIES

Today, many of us appreciate the awesome attributes of trees, but travel back through history, stripping away the clutter of modern life, and you can see that these remarkable plants seemed even more impressive in the past. The oldest living things in a community, they provided vital resources, towered over us, and many species even miraculously died and came back to life again each year. Giving thanks to these plants for their gifts and leaving them offerings in return in the hope that they continued to provide was a natural act of reverence.

But tree worship is much more than that. Trees have a great presence – a spirit. Many groups of people have interacted with tree spirits in the past and still worship them today. For others, trees play an important part in the rituals that mark the turning of the seasons and the passage of their lives. In this chapter, we'll cross cultures to discover sacred trees, meet tree deities and discover how tree worship continues to offer people spiritual roots to this day.

✶ SACRED GROVES ✶

Many cultures throughout history have cultivated sacred groves - outdoor temples where people could worship and commune with the divine. Groves were so revered by the Romans that damaging their trees was an act punishable by death, and the Greeks, too, planted sacred spaces. Archaeologists explored the 2,000-year-old site of a cypress grove at the Temple of Zeus at Nemea, which has recently been replanted with cypress trees.

But it is the Celts who are most often associated with grove worship, and evidence of their peaceful ceremonial spaces - called *nemeton* - has been found across Europe. Druids would preside over rituals in groves, which were places of judgement, worship and thanksgiving. One of the chief goddesses worshipped was Nemetona, whose name translates as "she of the sacred grove." Often the sacred trees were oaks, which were particularly revered for their strength. In fact, one theory is that the word "Druid" comes from the Celtic word for oak, *duir*, which is also linked to the idea that the oak could provide a doorway into the spiritual world.

We have limited written evidence for what rituals took place in these ancient spaces, but one account describes the harvesting by Druids of mistletoe for ceremonial use. This plant's ability to grow on oaks without rooting in the ground made it particularly magickal. In a time when people's lives were so strongly connected to natural cycles and were at the mercy of the elements, it's easy to see how a reverence for these powers could be enacted through tree worship in these sacred spaces.

Today, neopagans also cultivate groves and use these natural places for meditation, spell work and ceremonies that mark the passage of the seasons and their lives. There is plenty of advice online regarding planting your own grove (see *The Order of Bards, Ovates and Druids* in Further Reading on pages 124–125). As many people want to rediscover a lost connection with the natural world and its rhythms, spending time in a grove could be the perfect solution.

✦ GROVES ACROSS AFRICA ✦

Across Africa, many communities carry out tree worship or rituals centered on trees. For the semi-nomadic Nuer of South Sudan, where there are comparatively few trees, even the tree's shade is considered to be a sacred spirit-being.

In other areas, groves are a focal point for local worship. It's estimated, for example, that there are over 50,000 sacred groves in modern-day Burkina Faso. These spaces would originally have been heavily wooded with African teak and bark cloth trees, although fewer trees remain today. For the Bwaba people, the type of tree is less important than its location in the grove. Many groves have a "tree that matters" – sacred because it grows above the place where rituals, including divination and worship, are carried out. The groves' trees are revered for both practical and spiritual reasons – they give shade while ceremonies take place beneath them and are also a sign of the strength of the supernatural energy present in the sacred space.

It is strictly forbidden to damage or harvest any part of a grove, and so these places have become vital sites for biodiversity; the animals that live there – "children of

the grove" - are also protected. In Ghana, too, groves are preserved and honored as they are believed to be the dwelling places of the gods. They are visited for ancestor worship and by the local spiritual leader and his assistants, who will pray on behalf of the community and gather herbs and plants for traditional medicine. These wooded areas often include streams, so the water course is protected, too. Environmental groups have realized the importance of not just these spaces as sites of ecological significance but of the vast wealth of local knowledge of the flora and fauna amassed by the people who curate them.

DEITY – IROKO-MAN

The towering iroko tree is native to West Africa, where its leaves, bark and roots play an important role in traditional medicine. The tree is revered for these healing qualities and symbolizes a connection to ancestral spirits, serving as a sacred site for ceremonies.

For the Yoruba people, the tree is home to Iroko-man, a god who lives in the tree's lush canopy. Iroko-man is believed to have the power to grant wishes, and people may seek his wisdom when settling disputes. The trunk of the iroko tree is home to a host of spirits who must stop him from descending to earth, for any human who looks Iroko-man in the eye will be driven mad and die.

It is also believed that anyone who fells an iroko tree will meet with bad luck since Iroko-man's spirit is trapped in the wood. In fact, if you enter a house built of iroko timber and listen carefully, you may hear Iroko-man creaking and groaning in the walls.

✶ THE KARAM TREE FESTIVAL ✶

The Karam festival is a harvest celebration sacred to diverse tribal peoples in Jharkhand and Jhargram, West Bengal. It involves the worship of the holy tree, the karam (a type of teak), which symbolizes fertility and prosperity.

The ceremony begins when a group of Karam dancers go to the forest to pay tribute to the tree and cut one of its branches, which they carry back to the village while drumming, singing and dancing. The sacred branch is anointed with rice beer and milk, then set up in the center of the dancing area, where it is decorated with garlands of flowers. Everyone gathers to hear the retelling of the legend of Karam, the nature deity, and the celebrations continue through the night: feasting, dancing and singing to the beat of the mandar drum.

DEITY – DRYADS

Many different cultures describe trees as having a spirit or specific energy. In Sweden, it was believed that the forest nymph known as *Skogsrå* (Mistress of the Forest) would appear as a beautiful woman from the front but a rotten tree from behind. In the Black Forest in Germany, forest spirits were believed to protect the woods, allowing safe passage to travelers carrying walking sticks carved in their shape.

Perhaps the most common type of tree spirit known today in the West is the dryad. The word comes from Greek mythology, where it was used to describe nymphs that dwelled in oak trees. Other trees were said to be inhabited by spirits of different names; walnut tree spirits were called caryatids, for example. More recently, though, the term has broadened and applies to the spirit of an individual tree or grove, which people can tune in to if they take the time. By meditating with a tree, a person can contact its spirit and tap into its experience, discovering that different dryads have different energies and wisdom to impart.

TREE DEFENSES

Trees may be rooted to the spot, but that doesn't mean they can't defend themselves. Prickly leaves are an obvious method. Holly trees produce them when they're grazed, which is why you see them on lower branches.

Trees under attack from insects can send signals to neighbors through the wood wide web (see page 27), prompting them to produce defensive compounds. Others release tannins into their leaves to make them taste unappealing; beeches do this when they detect roe deer saliva. An acacia tree being grazed by a giraffe will use the same trick, releasing ethylene gas to warn its neighbors to do the same.

Some trees employ insect bodyguards to defend them from caterpillars. The Ecuador laurel produces sticky sap which becomes honeydew. This draws in ants, who nip at the caterpillars until they roll off the leaves. Pines use a grislier method of defense, releasing pheromones to attract parasitic wasps!

And some trees need to defend themselves against other plants: guavas can shed their bark to stop competitive vines getting a grip on their branches.

THE GLASTONBURY THORN

Legend has it that the lone hawthorn tree which stood for centuries atop a hillside overlooking Glastonbury, England, was planted by a saint – Joseph of Arimathea. It is said that Joseph traveled to this hilltop with the Holy Grail, following the burial of Christ. He drove his staff into the earth and the Holy Thorn sprang up in its place.

Most species of hawthorn only blossom in May, but, unusually, the Glastonbury thorn has two blooming seasons, and bursts into flower at Christmastime, too. When the tree was seen to bloom on Christmas Day, it was thought to be a miracle. The Holy Thorn became a symbol of Christianity and attracted crowds of worshippers every year.

The Holy Thorn has had a chequered past, though: the original tree was seen as a symbol of superstition by Cromwell's troops and cut down during the 1640s. (It is said that the man who swung the axe was blinded by the tree's thorns.) Fortunately, local folk kept cuttings of the tree and several descendants of it survive, including the Holy Thorn at Glastonbury Abbey and another at St John's Church.

A replacement tree was planted at the original site in 1952 and continued to attract visitors, both Christian and, more recently, pagan. (The hawthorn is seen as a symbol of fertility and new life - see page 13.) Unfortunately, this tree was vandalized in 2010, and its replacement vandalized in 2012, but a new tree was planted in 2022 in honor of King Charles III.

One tradition linked to the original Holy Thorn continues to this day. Every Christmas, since the days of Charles I, a cutting has been taken from a Holy Thorn and sent to the monarch as a symbol of the link between the royal family, the church and Glastonbury. Today, tradition dictates that the oldest child at the local school cuts a budded branch, which is blessed then sent to the monarch to decorate their Christmas dining table.

✶ SMOKING CEREMONIES ✶

Smoking rituals are carried out by many Indigenous Australian and Torres Strait Islander communities and are one of the oldest ceremonies still in use today. The rituals usually involve smouldering leaves - often eucalyptus or Berrigan emu bush - to produce a cleansing smoke that will ward off bad spirits. Different groups have different traditions, but ceremonies may be held to mark out the life stages from birth, through initiation, to Sorry Business (death). Smoke is used to help a deceased person's spirit to return to Country, and the ritual may also include using branches to sweep away the person's connection with the living world.

Smoking rituals are also used for healing - emu bush leaves have antimicrobial properties - and for cleansing spaces and objects. The ritual is usually led by a community Elder, and either a fire is made from tree bark in a pit, or coals are placed in a vessel called a coolamon, and green leaves are placed on top of it to produce the smoke.

DEITY – THE ELDER TREE MOTHER

In Danish folk tradition, every elder tree is sacred and is inhabited by a spirit called Hyldemoer, the Elder Tree Mother. She guards the tree and should anyone take her wood without asking permission, she will haunt the unfortunate pilferer. This explains why it's considered unlucky to bring elder wood into your home.

The Elder Tree Mother can be glimpsed on moonlit nights, appearing beside the tree, wearing a black dress and a white shawl. The correct greeting, should you need to chop some elder branches yourself is, "Give me some of your wood, then I will give you some of mine when it grows in the forest." If Hyldemoer remains silent, you have permission to go ahead. The sacred tree can grant you another special gift: stand beneath it at midnight on Midsummer's Eve and you may well see the King of Fairyland and his retinue ride past!

✶ WICCAN TREE WORSHIP ✶

Modern-day pagans center many of their rituals on trees. They may carry out rituals in groves or choose specific woods for magickal tools. Sacred activities are often linked to the turning of the seasons. Depending on personal choice, celebrations for the eight seasonal festivals, known as sabbats, could include:

YULE – WINTER SOLSTICE (20–22 DECEMBER*)

Burning a Yule log to bring light and protection into the home, and displaying evergreen wreaths to honor nature in the darkest season.

IMBOLC – THE RETURN OF LIGHT (1 FEBRUARY)

Lighting fires to celebrate the goddess Brigid and fashioning Brigid's crosses from reeds.

OSTARA – SPRING EQUINOX (19–21 MARCH)

A ritual spring-clean: brushing away negativity with a birch-twig besom.

*Dates in brackets are for the northern hemisphere. For example, Yule in the southern hemisphere falls on 20–22 June.

BELTANE – CELEBRATION OF FERTILITY (1 MAY)

Lighting a sacred "belfire" and writing wishes on ribbons and tying them to trees.

LITHA – SUMMER SOLSTICE (20–22 JUNE)

A celebration of the oak, as the Oak King has ruled over the first part of the year, and now the Holly King will take over. Oak bonfires are lit on Midsummer's Eve and people gather to welcome the dawn.

LUGHNASADH – FIRST HARVEST (1 AUGUST)

Eating and sharing berries (and other gifts of the harvest) and giving thanks.

MABON – AUTUMN EQUINOX (21–24 SEPTEMBER)

Celebrating the goddess Persephone with a pomegranate ritual and casting banishing spells using fallen leaves.

SAMHAIN – HONORING PASSED SOULS (31 OCTOBER)

Rituals using incense (made from tree resin and bark) to mark the passing of loved ones and remember them, and to cleanse and prepare for Wiccan New Year (1 November).

READING THE RINGS

Most people know that you can tell the age of a tree by counting the number of rings in a cross-section of its trunk (a process called dendrochronology), but tree rings also give us a wealth of information about the history of the tree and of the climate, too. In very old trees, this data may predate climate records. Scientists can extract a thin sliver of the trunk to analyze without harming the tree.

If you come across a fallen tree, try counting the rings to determine its age. Each light-colored ring (formed in spring/early summer) is followed by a darker ring (formed in late summer/autumn), so count each pair as one year. Wider rings indicate a warmer year with plenty of rainfall; narrow rings show a colder or drier season. You might notice other details, such as black scarring from a fire, marks from an insect infestation, or rings that show more growth on one side of the trunk than the other, showing that the tree had started to lean.

THE COTTONWOOD AND THE WHITE PINE

The Lakota (Sioux) revere the cottonwood tree, as for them it embodies the Great Spirit, Wakan Tanka. Every year, communities hold a Sun Dance ceremony with a cottonwood tree at its center. The ritual is a time of renewal, when people come together to sing and dance to traditional drumming. The tree may be decorated with streamers of different colors, representing the different points of the compass. Cottonwoods are significant because, when the twigs are broken in the right place, they reveal a five-pointed star at their center, earning them the title "Tree of Life" (see page 59).

The Tree of Peace, a white pine, has become a symbol of peace for the Haudenosaunee (Iroquois) Confederacy. Originally the tree, with its needles in bundles of five, was symbolic of peace between five warring nations. The longevity of these pine trees represents the passing down of this peace through the generations, and Tree of Peace ceremonies are held today to symbolize this and acknowledge the importance of First Nations heritage.

DEITY – KODAMA AND KINUSHI

In the Shinto religion, people worship many *kami*: deities or spirits that often inhabit natural phenomena, such as the waves, rocks or, of course, trees. Tree spirits are known in Japanese as *kodama*. They don't inhabit every tree, but those trees that do have them are protected and often marked with a *shimenawa* rope to prevent anyone cutting them down by mistake. (These ropes are used to mark purified, sacred spaces in Shintoism.)

Worship of *kami* takes different forms, but in some villages there is an annual festival for *kodama-san*, in which the villagers give thanks to the tree spirits and ask for forgiveness for taking wood throughout the year. In other areas, people create shrines at the foot of trees and pray to them.

In Okinawa, the tree spirits are called *kinushi*, and you may encounter one at night; if you hear the sound of a falling tree, it is said to be a *kinushi* crying out.

THE FESTIVAL OF GREEN GEORGE

St George's Day (23 April) is celebrated across Europe to welcome in the fertile season for those who live off the land. Traditionally, in Romania and Slovenia, people mark the day with a festival centered on a willow that is set up, rather like a maypole, and decorated with flowers and leaves. Houses and gates throughout the village are also decorated with green branches.

The festival celebrates Green George, a version of the Green Man (see page 68), and a young boy from the village traditionally dresses as him in green leaves and foliage. He performs a ritual, hammering three iron nails into the willow and then casting them into the stream, to attract enough rainfall for the year's crops. Another tradition is for pregnant women to lay a piece of clothing under the willow and return in the morning to see whether a leaf has fallen on it overnight. If so, it is said, they will have an easy labor!

THE KAURI TREES OF WAIPOUA

Two mighty kauri trees stand guard in Waipoua Forest, New Zealand. These trees, Te Matua Ngahere (Father of the Forest) and Tāne Mahuta (Lord of the Forest), are sacred to the Māori people, who sing a song of greeting and praise when visiting them. Tāne Mahuta is the son of the Earth Mother and Sky Father, and brought light to the world by pushing against the sky and earth, separating them. He stands today at over 51 metres tall (167 feet), keeping them apart.

Aside from the two giant kauri trees in Waipoua, groves of kauri are cultivated as sacred spaces and, in the past, the bones of the dead were placed in hollows in these trees so that their spirit could occupy them.

In Māori tradition, the life force of a particular area, known as its *mauri*, can be condensed into special stones. The *mauri* stone from a forest, waterway or other sacred area was often used for protection, and today *mauri* stones may be used by Māori for grounding and to benefit their mental health in a stressful environment.

DEITY – NANG TA-KHIAN

In Thailand, ancient animism beliefs live on in the worship of tree spirits, known as *nang mai.* Of these spirits, none is more revered than Nang Ta-khian, who takes the form of a beautiful Thai woman and inhabits takian trees. These tall trees were considered to be portals to the underworld in Thai mythology and are sacred to this day. They're rarely cut down, for fear of upsetting Nang Ta-khian, although monks may occasionally carry out a ceremony requesting the spirit's permission to do so.

Nang Ta-khian is a benevolent spirit, protecting travelers and pregnant women alike, as well as bringing visitors luck in the lottery, in return for the garlands of brightly colored silks they tie around the tree's trunk. But like many tree spirits, Nang Ta-khian is said to have a dark side. If people do not pay her due respect, she will fill the forest with her shrieks of rage, and she may also be heard singing to lure unsuspecting men into her embrace then engulfing them into the tree's trunk.

CHAPTER FIVE:

TREE MAGICK, RITUALS AND SPELLS

It's easy to connect with the peaceful and powerful energy of trees, whether it's by meditating beneath them or using their gifts in your rituals. The benefits of connecting with nature in this way are huge: by tuning in to the rhythms of the natural world, you open yourself up to its healing power.

In this chapter, you'll discover how trees can be used in divination, learn how to make a seasonal altar and experiment with spells to bring some tree magick into your life. Remember to be respectful of the gifts nature offers you (perhaps leaving a gift in return), and to use your intuition to adapt these suggestions to suit you. Spell work magnifies your intentions, so the more relevant the spell is to you, the more effective it will be.

Some rituals suggest you start by casting a circle: if outside, you could use bird seed to do this; otherwise set your sacred space by simply walking through the four compass points in the outline of a circle, starting from North.

✶ MAGICKAL TOOLS ✶

Magickal tools enhance and focus the spellcaster's energy, and using different types of wood is a wonderful way to bring a tree's specific qualities to your rituals. Any tools you work with should be cleansed and charged before use. A ritual to cleanse a tool might include smudging it with sage or incense. You could then charge it by leaving it in moonlight, for example, and reciting a simple incantation before its first use.

WANDS

Wands are used to draw down energy from the sky or to draw grounding energy up from the earth to direct your intentions, and to draw sigils in the air. You might have different wands for different purposes: birch for creative spells; rowan for protection spells and casting your circle, for example. You can buy handmade wands at local fairs, where you may find you're attracted to one in particular. Alternatively, make and decorate your own. You could use a fallen twig from a favorite tree; sandpaper away any rough edges, and decorate and varnish it if you like.

STAFFS

You may find yourself drawn to a sturdy staff when walking in the woods and decide to use this in your magick work. Staffs can be held when casting spells or used to mark out the area where you will carry out a ritual.

INCENSE

Made from tree bark or resin, incense brings a sense of ceremony to your rituals, and the different scents add different qualities to your spells. Incense can also be used to purify an area before spellcasting and to cleanse magickal items.

BESOM

Perhaps the most obvious wooden tool for a Wiccan, these brooms, usually made from birch twigs, can be used in spell work to ceremonially cleanse negative energy as well as for literally sweeping a space.

OTHER TOOLS

You can also add the magick of trees to your rituals by using a wooden dowsing rod, pendulum, pendulum board, athame (ceremonial knife) or chalice.

AUTUMN BERRIES AND LEAVES

When trees shed their leaves in the autumn, it's a good time to think about letting go of anything that no longer serves you, and plan new projects for the season ahead. This ritual works nicely on an autumn evening when you're gathered around the dinner table. It will help you and your loved ones focus on the things you want to leave behind and set new goals instead.

You'll need a bowl of autumn leaves and a bowl of berries or chopped fruit. First, pass the leaves around the table. Each person takes one, names something they wish to leave behind and then drops the leaf to the floor. Keep going until everybody has "shed" all their issues - you may need quite a big bowl of leaves! Now pass the fruit around and encourage everyone to name something they would like to welcome into their life and eat a berry or a piece of fruit to symbolize their new blessings.

THE SCIENCE OF *SHINRIN-YOKU*

Although the science behind forest bathing has only been around for a few decades, it confirms something people have known for much longer: spending time among trees is beneficial for our health. Based on studies carried out in Japan in the 1980s, *shinrin-yoku* encourages people to spend time immersing themselves in a forest environment, a practice that lowers blood pressure and levels of cortisol (the body's primary stress hormone) and improves mood. Incredibly, forest bathing also boosts our immune systems: trees release phytoncides, natural compounds with antimicrobial properties that increase the production of NK (natural killer) cells, which help us combat disease.

Forest bathing appeals to all our senses, from the immune-boosting scents of the essential oils trees release to the natural soundscape of birdsong and rustling leaves. The visual appeal of the forest is calming, too. Take a slow and mindful walk through a forest, sit a while and breathe in the benefits, which can last up to a month after your visit.

✶ TREE DIVINATION ✶

The ancient Greeks and Romans often studied nature for signs and portents. Trees have long been associated with wisdom, so using them for divination is an obvious choice. With practice, you can look to bark, twigs, leaves or rings to gain insight into your situation.

LEAVES

If you need guidance when choosing between two or more options, select the relevant number of large leaves and write one choice on each – or nominate a leaf for each option. On a breezy day, cast a circle and meditate on your decision for a moment, asking mother nature for guidance. Place your leaves in the circle, saying:

Whichever choice is best for me,
Let the leaf remain, so mote it be.

Wait for the wind to scatter the leaves until just one remains. If there's no breeze, you could release the leaves above the circle and declare that the leaf which lands closest to the center holds your answer.

BARK

Find a tree with interesting, irregular bark and stand before it, eyes closed, meditating on your question and asking the tree for guidance. Open your eyes and examine the bark, looking for any shapes or patterns that stand out to you. Run your fingers over them and consider how they could relate to your question. Here are some suggestions of what different shapes could mean:

- **Circles:** Be patient, things will fall into place "as the wheel turns" (at the right time).
- **Triangles:** Creativity, wisdom and positive thinking are required.
- **Squares:** Prioritize home, safety and financial security.
- **A fork:** You need to be decisive to progress.
- **Letters:** You may see the initial of a person relevant to your query.

Watch out, too, for repeated patterns, which may reveal a number relevant to your issue.

GREET A TREE

Spending time with trees benefits your mind, body and spirit, and is a wonderful way to rebuild your connection with nature. This ritual shows you how to share a mindful moment with a tree you admire.

1. Start by greeting your tree – lay your palm against its bark or your forehead against its trunk. Close your eyes and take some slow breaths as you connect with the tree's calming and positive energy.
2. Now find a comfortable place to settle and let your tree support you. It will happily do so. Lean with your back against its trunk or lie with your head cradled in its roots and gaze up at its canopy overhead.

3. Spend a while admiring the treasures your tree has to offer – the sight of its leaves jeweled with sunlight contrasting with the sky above, or the sigh of the wind through its branches. Breathe in the sharp scent of its foliage or the loamy soil at its roots. Trace the whorls of its bark beneath your fingertips and sense its aura of wisdom and strength.
4. When it's time to leave, you may like to give your tree a hug – there's something very reassuring about wrapping your arms around a tree's trunk and feeling tiny in comparison. Thank your tree for sharing its energy with you, and for all the other services these grand guardians of the landscape offer us.

MAKE AN OAK SPELL POUCH

Spell pouches can be made for many magickal purposes. This one includes objects that will boost confidence and strength, but you could use different items to create a bag for protection, love or positivity, for example. Do a little research to see which leaves, seeds, crystals, colors, symbols and herbs would suit your purpose.

You will need:

- A small red or orange bag*
- A felt-tip pen
- An acorn and an oak leaf
- A carnelian or tiger's eye crystal

*If you're handy with a needle and thread, you could make your own cloth bag and even embroider a rune or symbol on it for added potency.

URUZ
Strength

Method:

1. Find a quiet place and gather all your items. (Sitting under an oak would be perfect for this, but don't worry if that's not practical.)
2. Picture a mighty oak and take a moment to evoke the energy of the tree. Let it flow through you as you draw Uruz (the rune for strength; see above) on your leaf. Pick up your items in turn and feel the oak's energy flowing into each one before placing it in the bag.
3. Finally, say aloud, "May this charm bag bring me the strength and protection of the oak." Hold it in both hands as you imbue it with protective energy.
4. Carry your charm bag with you or hang it up in your home or car.

EXPLORE YOUR OWN GROVE

This ritual is a lovely way to drift off to sleep at night. The beauty of it is that you can adjust your grove dream world to suit your needs every time you visit.

1. Start by relaxing your muscles and taking some slow, deep breaths.
2. Picture yourself walking down a path through a meadow toward a wood. It's a warm day and the meadow is alive with wildflowers. Soon you find yourself entering the green, welcoming forest. Patches of sunlight pool on the mosses, and clumps of woodland flowers are at your feet.
3. The path emerges into a glade. You're welcomed by a circle of trees around the edge, and can feel their warm, peaceful energy as you pass them. This is

your grove. The grass is soft and inviting and there is a clear pool at the glade's center.

4. Now explore... If you need grounding, you might sit with your back to a sturdy tree and dig your toes into the loamy soil at its roots. If your thoughts are muddled, peer into the surface of the pool, reflecting on any images you see there. Perhaps you need to shed some negative thoughts? Sit up in the boughs of a tree, watching autumn leaves fall away beneath you. Or if you're feeling afraid, create a cozy space inside the hollow trunk of a large tree, and curl up there.
5. Let your imagination take the lead - with practice you'll find that your subconscious will show you what you need to find.

MAKING A SEASONAL ALTAR

Your altar can be a place where you reflect, set intentions and work spells. Changing it to represent the Wheel of the Year is a lovely way to maintain your connection with nature, and incorporating seasonal gifts from trees is perfect for this. Whenever you go for a walk, keep an eye out for natural items that you can use to decorate your sacred space(s). You could set up an outdoor shrine to the Green Man, too.

Start by burning incense to cleanse your chosen space. Then add your magickal tools, tarot or oracle cards, and any items that represent the trees and spiritual beings or animals you're drawn to. Now add your seasonal touches:

SPRING

Candle colors: yellow, pale green

Natural gifts: seeds in a dish, a posy of spring flowers or greenery, painted eggs, twigs, images of the Green Man

SUMMER

Candle colors: orange, red, gold

Natural gifts: a posy of buttercups, a daisy chain, shells, hag stones (pebbles with a naturally occurring hole through them), an offering of milk, images of bees, fresh herbs, large green leaves, a stalk of corn or wheat

AUTUMN

Candle colors: orange, bronze, brown, blue

Natural gifts: fallen leaves, acorns, conkers, pumpkin seeds, pine cones, seed heads, berries, nuts

WINTER

Candle colors: red, dark green, silver, gold

Natural gifts: twigs, sprigs of holly and other evergreens, a whole nutmeg, cinnamon sticks, spices, nuts, oranges

A WISHING SPELL

This spell uses the energy of a tree to magnify your intentions and combines two ancient forms of spellcasting: knot-tying and color magick.

You will need:

- A tree
- A small bag of birdseed
- A pen
- A colored ribbon (pink for love; red for passion and strength; white for peace; green for luck and money; blue for communication and healing; yellow for happiness and friendships; orange for creativity and career)

Method:

1. First, select your tree: you could seek out a species associated with your request - apple for a love wish, for example - but choosing one that you're drawn to is just as effective. Spend a few moments greeting your tree.
2. Walk round your tree in a clockwise direction, sprinkling a rough circle of seed on the ground around it. (You're leaving an edible gift while also casting your circle.)
3. Sit in the circle and focus on your wish. Picture your ideal outcome as clearly as you can.
4. Write your wish on the ribbon, then tie it to one of the branches of the tree, binding the magick, and saying:

   I ask this favor, sacred tree
   Grant this wish, so mote it be.

5. Close your circle by walking round the tree once more in an anticlockwise direction, trailing your hand around its trunk, and sending gratitude to the tree.

MAKE YOUR OWN RUNES

People have used runic symbols for divination for over 2,000 years. Making your own runes gives you the chance to personalize them and add your own magickal energy to the mix.

You will need:

- A rune chart
- 24 pre-bought wooden discs (or cut your own)
- Paint and a brush, a permanent marker or a pyrography tool
- A cloth bag

Method:

1. Start by choosing which runes you would like to use. The Elder Futhark is a good choice. It is the oldest runic alphabet in use today, and its symbols are versatile and practical for readings. If you prefer a tree theme, use the 20 Ogham symbols instead.
2. If you're cutting your own discs, the branch of a fruit tree is the best choice of wood. Ask the tree's permission and cut discs of roughly the same size. Prepare them by sanding off any rough edges and wiping with a damp cloth. Then inscribe each rune in turn, meditating on its meaning as you do so.
3. Once completed, you'll need to cleanse your runes by smudging them with incense, and then charge them for use. A ritual to do this could involve placing them on your altar to one side of a lit candle. Pass each rune over the flame in turn, saying its name and meaning aloud as you do so.
4. Keep your runes safe in a cloth bag. A good way to start working with them is to hold a question in your mind as you draw a rune out of the bag for guidance, or try a simple three-rune reading, drawing one each for the past, present and future of your situation.

A GROUNDING RITUAL

This visualization is very calming and is perfect for when you need to ground yourself. You can do this standing outside barefoot, but it is effective carried out anywhere and anywhen. Practice it often!

1. Take a moment to still yourself and settle into your space. Feel the earth, solid and firm, beneath you. Now imagine roots extending from your feet and anchoring you safely to the ground. Picture them threading down from your feet into the soil, past rocks, deeper and deeper. Perhaps their tips are touching an underground stream.
2. Next, stand up, straightening the core of your body as it takes on the strength of the trunk of a tree. Keep your shoulders and neck relaxed, but straighten your arms and wiggle your fingers – these are your branches, of course!

3. Breathe slowly and deeply into your abdomen. With every in-breath imagine positive, nourishing energy flowing up into you from the earth below. Let it spread up through your body. With every out-breath release any negativity or stress into the air around you and picture it dissipating into the atmosphere.
4. Once you feel calm, send your awareness down to the tips of your roots and picture them reaching out and meeting others in a vast network under the ground. In this way, you are connected to your friends, family and all life on earth.
5. Enjoy this sensation of belonging and send feelings of love and peace to those around you before gently returning to everyday life.

✶ FAREWELL ✶

We've reached the end of our journey through the magickal world of trees, but hopefully your relationship with them is just beginning. Folklore is a rich and fascinating area, and there is so much to explore. And, of course, there is plenty more to learn about the amazing biology of trees, as new discoveries are being made all the time. Take a look at the Further Reading section (pages 124–125) for some suggestions of tree-based books and podcasts to enjoy.

Our millennia-old relationship with trees should be mutually beneficial, and there's plenty we can do to give something back to our leafy companions, whether it's protecting trees in your local area, encouraging friends and family to care for them, or supporting a tree charity – even sharing posts on social media can help.

There are also many ways you can bring tree magick into your everyday life: practicing and developing your own rituals, visiting the woods and meditating with a favorite tree, sketching them, photographing them throughout the year, finding a place to display their gifts in your home... However you choose to celebrate them, we hope that your path ahead is lined with many

marvellous trees, and that you find time to pause awhile and consider their magickal stories.

✶ FURTHER READING ✶

BOOKS

Danu Forest, *Celtic Tree Magick* (2014)
Fiona Stafford, *The Long, Long Life of Trees* (2016)
Jacqueline Memory Paterson, *Tree Wisdom* (1996)
Lisa Chamberlain, *Wicca Tree Magick* (2019)
Peter Wohlleben, *The Hidden Life of Trees* (2018)
Rachel Patterson, *A Witch for Every Season* (2022)
Thomas Pakenham, *Meetings with Remarkable Trees* (1996)

PODCASTS

Branch Out, Botanic Gardens of Sydney, Vanessa Fuchs
Comfy Cozy Witch Podcast, Jennie Blonde
Completely Arbortrary, Casey Clapp and Alex Crowson
Myths and Legends, Carissa Weiser and Jason Weiser
Rooted by Nature, Samantha Sear
Woodland Walks, the Woodland Trust

WEBSITES

Arbor Day Foundation - *www.arborday.org*

OBOD - The Order of Bards, Ovates and Druids - *www.druidry.org*

One Tree Planted - *www.onetreeplanted.org*

The Folklore Society - *www.folklore-society.com*

The Rainforest Trust - *www.rainforesttrust.org*

The Tree Council - *www.treecouncil.org.uk*

The Woodland Trust - *www.woodlandtrust.org.uk*

THE LITTLE BOOK OF FOLKLORE

Kitty Greenbrown

ISBN: 978-1-59003-589-4

The Little Book of Folklore explores the magical and mystical tales that have shaped the British Isles. Filled with stories of iconic characters - such as Robin Hood and Merlin, as well as tales of the Green Man, giants, and witches - this beautiful little book also explores modern customs and traditions grounded in folklore, such as May Day and Halloween, the deep connection between folklore and nature, and the historical context surrounding folklore and the insight it gives us into the beliefs of British and Irish people in times gone by.

THE LITTLE BOOK OF MOON MAGIC

Francis Nightingale

ISBN: 978-1-59003-556-6

This is the perfect book for anyone charmed and intrigued by the wonder of the moon. In this guide you will find myths and legends about the moon, guidance on how to perform rituals that can help you tap into the moon's power, and moon meditations that can enrich your life.

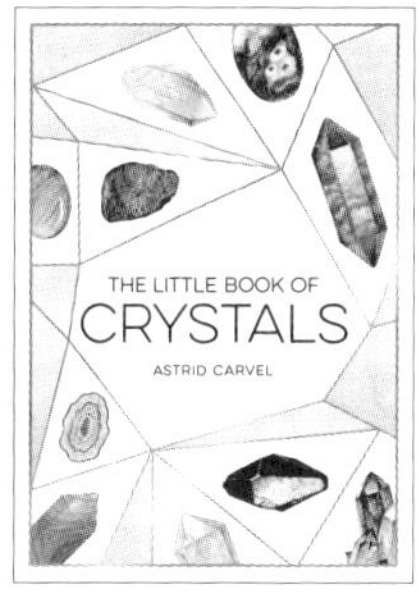

THE LITTLE BOOK OF CRYSTALS

Astrid Carvel

ISBN: 978-1-59003-557-3

This guide introduces over forty essential crystals and their unique properties. You will discover how crystals work, how to select and maintain your crystals, how to make use of their power in everyday life, basic techniques for crystal meditation, how to balance your chakras using crystals, and a guide to birthstones.

Based on the symbolism of the wheel, Red Wheel offers books and divination decks from a variety of traditions. We aim to provide the ideas, information, and innovative approaches to help you develop your own spiritual path.

Please visit our website,
WWW.REDWHEELWEISER.COM,
to learn more about our full range of titles

IMAGE CREDITS

Cover and throughout © ekosuwandono/Shutterstock.com, © In Art/Shutterstock.com, © Neliakott/Shutterstock.com, © lyubava.21/Shutterstock.com; p.8 © M.Svetlana/Shutterstock.com; p.11 © aksol/Shutterstock.com; p.12 © Anastasia Lembrik/Shutterstock.com; p.15 © Evgenii Doljenkov/Shutterstock.com; p.21 © OlgaChernyak/Shutterstock.com; p.53 © Croisy/Shutterstock.com, © Tanya Sid/Shutterstock.com; p.65 © RogelioDioArt/Shutterstock.com; p.68 © patrimonio designs ltd/Shutterstock.com; p.70 © Good Shrek/Shutterstock.com; p.77 © EDE design/Shutterstock.com, © kateluck/Shutterstock.com; p.83 © aksol/Shutterstock.com; p.85 © Val_Iva/Shutterstock.com; p.91 © Yevheniia Lytvynovych/Shutterstock.com; pp.108–120 © robin.ph/Shutterstock.com; p.110 © Lickomicko/Shutterstock.com